WHEN THE CHIPS ARE DOWN

WHEN THE CHIPS ARE DOWN

by
SAMMY O. JOSEPH

PULSE PUBLISHING HOUSE

When the Chips are DOWN

© 2013 Sammy O. Joseph

Published in the United Kingdom by
PULSE Publishing House
Box 15129
Birmingham
England B45 5DJ

pulsepublishinghouse@harvestways.org

All rights reserved. No part of this publication may be
reproduced, stored in a retrieval system, or be transmitted, in any
form, or by any means, mechanical, electronic, photocopying or
otherwise without prior written consent of the publisher.

Bible quotes are from the King James Version
of the Bible unless otherwise stated.

Amplified quotes are from the Amplified Bible,
© copyright 1995 by The Zondervan Corporation
and The Lockman Foundation.

Cover photo credit: Dr. Christian Sasse;
© copyrights 2013 *PULSE Publishing House*.

Cover design and typesetting
by *PULSE Publishing House*, England.
Printed in England.

ISBN 978-0-9567298-9-7

Contents

Acknowledgement		*i*
Dedication		*iii*
Preface		*v*
Chapter 1	Introduction	1
Chapter 2	Wholesome Wellness within your Camp	7
Chapter 3	When the Chips Come Down	19
Chapter 4	Four proven, Life-sustenance Principles	45
Chapter 5	The Ungrateful Son	85
References		*89*
Worship with Us		*91*
Become a Vision Partner		*94*
Contact Addresses		*96*

Acknowledgement

On behalf of *PULSE Publishing House*, I do gratefully acknowledge my German-Canadian friend, Dr. Christian Sasse whose relentless love and passion for vivid capture of the bald eagles had birthed this book's perfect *backcover-shot!* Thanks so much Christian, for demonstrating your passion for the entire world to benefit from!

To a fine gentleman, our dear Bryn Davies, a graphic illustrator with eyes for details; a man whose finesse of a contribution was greatly missed on my last project the *'APPRECIABLE Gifts'* during which time he had been bereaved of his loving father, Ian!

To Dr. & Pastor (Mrs.) Creflo Dollar; thank you both for righteously dividing the Word of Truth, over the years, with focused determination such as the bald eagle's!

A worthy acknowledgement of Dr. Mike Murdock must be made for his exceptional insight into teaching on the wisdom of God.

And last but not the least, to the *five quivers* the Almighty GOD entrusted unto me to nurture and supervise with dedicated, watchful, 'eagle-like focus' – who while being raised had not been spared occasional probing stares from those big, beautiful, bulging eyeballs of mine: *my* Gabriella, *my* David, *my* Daniel, *my* Priscilla and *'our'* apostle Paul! Thank you all for taking turns to work with me on this book project – and encouraging me so dearly to focus on the *ministry* unto which I've been called! I am proud of you all – and so is our Big Daddy, God!

Dedication

This project is hereby dedicated to all the *eagle-beings* out there who recognize the heights they have been divinely equipped to attain - and *are* constantly mounting up and soaring, in spite of the ubiquitous, ever-present force of gravity!

I have also dedicated it to those who currently tread gingerly the 'valley of shadows', in weakness; those maturing eagles who are preening their feathers and molting their flesh in readiness and a collective strong anticipation of new outbursts of energies and leases of life – that would enable them soar unto new, greater heights.

May you indeed soar!

Preface

Sometime in November 2012, after I'd awaited in vain, word from our publishing team on the exact release-date of my newest release at the time: *'Appreciable Gifts'*, the Spirit of God had begun moving upon the team and I to start releasing 'snippets 'of my teachings via video clips uploaded onto *YouTube*.

Possessed by an age-long perfectionist trait, I'd first resisted the idea of adding a "new voice" unto the airwaves; an apparently unknown voice that had been bereft of post-recording 'make-overs', edits and general professional production embellishments like voice and acoustic fine-tuning, *intro*, *outro* – and the program's signature tune! In trepidation of the plainly obvious, I had reluctantly given my consent for world-wide web uploads – just once weekly!

Today, as I look back into the not-too distant successful outing of *'HarvestWays with Sammy Joseph'* on the *You Tube* – and the listeners' reports generated by our weekly broadcasts on Pan American Broadcasting Company's *Radio Pan Am* stationed in Pasadena, California and *Radio AFRICA* on 7190/15190 kHz shortwave in the 49 and 19 meter-bands respectively since March 7th, 2013; I cannot but be eternally grateful to the Spirit of the LORD Who had overwhelmed *my* imperfections – and had so blessed countless lives through those 'raw' files! *(Who says God still can't slay a giant by a faithful stone, cast in His name?)*

One of the best-loved teaching video clips which had challenged hearts most and elicited the strongest reactions from viewers and listeners across the world, bears the title of this *very* book: 'When the Chips are Down'.

Naturally, when trouble assails, we humans automatically become *seekers*. We seek to *know*, to *learn*, to *hear*: "All will be alright" in the midst of the storm! Fortunately there exists, undoubtedly, an ancient Book – the Bible – which re-assures us time and again of a God *"who is rich in mercy, for His great love, wherewith he loved us."*[1]

Based upon the deep lamentations of Prophet Jeremiah in the third chapter of his words of hope amidst hopelessness, I shall fully entrust unto the Holy Spirit *His* duty, to minister to you, through the printed words on these pages:

> *"And I said, My strength and my hope is perished from the LORD:*

Remembering mine affliction and my misery, the wormwood and the gall.

My soul hath them still in remembrance, and is humbled in me.

This I recall to my mind, therefore have I hope.

It is of the LORD's mercies that we are not consumed, because His compassions fail not.

They are new every morning: great is thy faithfulness.

The LORD is my portion, saith my soul; therefore will I hope in him.

The LORD is good unto them that wait for him, to the soul that seeketh him.

It is good that a man should both hope and quietly wait for the salvation of the LORD.

It is good for a man that he bear his yoke in his youth.

He sitteth alone and keepeth silence, because he hath borne it upon him.

He putteth his mouth in the dust; if so be there may be hope.

He giveth his cheek to him that smiteth him: he is filled full with reproach.

For the Lord will not cast off for ever:

But though he cause grief, yet will he have compassion according to the multitude of his mercies.

For he doth not afflict willingly nor grieve the children of men."

—LAMENTATIONS 3:18-33

1
INTRODUCTION

Link's Dysfunctional Family

In the *'HarvestWays with Sammy Joseph'* video message broadcast that had birthed this book's title, I had aptly made mention of Robert Swindells' epic, Carnegie Award-winning book, titled *'Stone Cold'*.

In that book, the author had described a dysfunctional Yorkshire family of the late '70's where father had run off with a younger receptionist – leaving behind his wife and two teen-aged children: daughter, Carole; eighteen and son, Link; fourteen respectively!

Not quite much later after this development, the late-thirties working-mother of two had found for a partner, a jobless, pot-bellied, lousy man in his fifties, called Vince.

WHEN THE CHIPS ARE DOWN

Vince had always wanted to be referred to as "Dad" – a wish the teenagers had abruptly ignored from the very onset!

Surprisingly as the months rolled on, loathsome Vince had started making un-becoming sexual advances and passes at Carole! Though Link had suspected his foul moves, neither he nor Carole had been able to convince *Mother* – a mother who had either fallen too grossly in love with, or had been too afraid of Vince – to confront his waywardness! So he had continued the callous, systematic violations of Carole even on a heightened scale.

With ever-turbulent topsy-turvy emotions within the young female teenager scarcely controllable, Carole, one afternoon had sat *Mother* down for a 'reality-check' discussion! She could have "braved up" to Mother's face but it all had ended in a noisy row: *Mother* had chosen sides – and Carol had walked out of the family home! She had sought refuge in the house of her 'get-away' boyfriend!

Link, her brother had now been left alone to shield and defend himself against an abusive step-dad Vince, who apparently now had glaringly transformed into a bully, a petty-thief on *Mother*'s stray notes, a gambler and a drunk – all to the denial of an oblivious woman whose emotions too, had fallen irreconcilably, apart!

INTRODUCTION

Angrier outbursts and rows had ensued between the two male inmates, oftener! Vince had become nastier by the day – and had begun to physically assault Link, slapping him on the face and banging his head against the wall, on occasions! One day, he had eventually locked him out of the house, and had prevented the mother from opening the door for her son to lodge. The younger inmate had been forced out of his rights; Link had ended up on the streets, homeless, in metropolitan London![1]

It was obviously undeniable: the *chips had come down* in each of those lives!

Further Tell-tale Signs of a Dysfunctional Person

If you felt unwell, you would visit the doctor! The medical practitioner would proceed to carry out a *diagnosis* which would most often include some preliminary questioning. Sometimes, only after a few questions have been asked – which if answered truthfully and with integrity – the root cause(s) of the illness(es) would be revealed based upon the depth of medical knowledge and experience of the examiner! In some cases, additional medical examinations may be mandatory! In that wise, they could further refer you to a specialist where more detailed medical examinations and diagnostic tests would be conducted. In most cases they would schedule you for a phlebotomist's appointment, who would simply take your blood specimen for the laboratory, in order that they may accurately *diagnose* the root-cause of your ailment!

In a similar token, because human beings generally are intrinsically plagued by *doubt* – accosted possibly by *unbelief*, Link's dysfunctional family-type apart, a few, tell-tale signs *should* bear an unflinching witness to anyone doubting whether or not what *season of life* they are undergoing, is a season the *'chips are down'*!

Just like a trained physician therefore, kindly allow me to use the scalpel of God's Spirit through Jeremiah's observations in his writing cited in *Lamentations 3*, to depict to you beyond every iota of doubt, the one whose *'chips are down'*. This person, male or female would definitely exhibit traits of:

- undeniable excruciating, first class experiences of affliction(s) *(verse 1)*;
- preference of darkness to light *(verse 2)*;
- probably experiencing – or having experienced degenerative functions of a physiological member *(verse 3)*;

INTRODUCTION

- strong feelings of being hedged in – and *not* easily able to envisage a way of escape out of despair *(verse 7)*;
- experiencing and documenting proofs of un-answered prayers which lead to bitterness of heart against God *(verse 8)*;
- prevalent crookedness – and the presence of willful sin(s) in their personal life *(verse 9)*;
- inconsolable feelings of loneliness, desolation and despondency *(verse 11)*; and,
- consistent dogged feelings of being a failure, a victim – or actually experiencing victimizations *(verses 12-14)*.

Other tell-tale signs of someone whose *chips are down* include:

- being filled with bitterness and gall *(verse 15)*;
- brokenness – and nursing a broken spirit *(verse 16)*;
- presence of turmoil after turmoil – and an absence of peace *(verse 17)*;
- presence of poverty, degradation and lack *(verse 17)*;
- presence of health risks, feelings of general lethargy and weakness; and finally,
- hopelessness and helplessness *(verse 18)*.

WHEN THE CHIPS ARE DOWN

Wow, what an overwhelming feeling it is to be deluged by all these happenings – and eventualities!

Now, when a soul faces such an immense pressure – or a combination of one or more of these many eventualities of life, what should they do? How would they be able to escape the *"net of the fowler"*?[2]

Find out on subsequent pages of the book!

2

WHOLESOME WELLNESS WITHIN YOUR CAMP

A person's quality of life can be fully measured. Both qualitatively and quantitatively! Now, only *you* will decide how *full* and *qualitative* you want your life to be!

Not everyone will experience exact same dysfunction as Link – or indeed, his family members. Some other individuals' experiences may prove to being far worse – or in some cases, just slightly better! But in spite of the struggles it will encounter, the human soul has an unquantifiable potential to arise from the depths of despair, overcome all odds – and emerge, triumphant!

This is my goal in this entire project: that my writing may encourage your soul to receive strength yet again and resonate with tremendous optimism in the face of the mountainous challenges it daily faces – or would face!

You can achieve wellness, within your camp; I mean *total* wellness – and it is my strong aim to show you *how*.

God wants it well; *totally* well – within *your* camp! He does *not* derive any pleasure in your grieving due to un-wellness. Un-wellness results from hurts of various kinds, broken promises, broken hearts; lack, illnesses, afflictions, generational curses, unmet aspirations, goals and desires.

Scripture admonishes:

> *"Let them shout for joy, and be glad, that favour my righteous cause: yea, let them say continually, Let the LORD be magnified, which hath pleasure in the prosperity of His servant."*
>
> —PSALMS 35:27

Here are a few more scriptures that strongly affirm the unshakeable truth that the Creator of the Universe desires your uncompromising total wellness:

WHOLESOME WELLNESS WITHIN YOUR CAMP

"And when they came to Marah, they could not drink of the waters of Marah, for they were bitter: therefore the name of it was called Marah.

And the people murmured against Moses, saying, What shall we drink?

And he cried unto the LORD; and the LORD shewed him a tree, which when he had cast into the waters, the waters were made sweet: there he made for them a statute and an ordinance, and there he proved them,

And said, If thou wilt diligently hearken to the voice of the LORD thy God, and wilt do that which is right in his sight, and wilt give ear to his commandments, and keep all his statutes, I will put none of these diseases upon thee, which I have put upon the Egyptians: for I am the LORD that healeth thee."

—EXODUS 15:23-26

"And ye shall serve the LORD your God, and he shall bless thy bread, and thy water; and I will take sickness away from the midst of thee.

There shall nothing cast their young, nor be barren, in thy land: the number of thy days I will fulfill.

WHEN THE CHIPS ARE DOWN

I will send my fear before thee, and will destroy all the people to whom thou shalt come, and I will make all thine enemies turn their backs onto thee."

—EXODUS 23:25-27

"Beloved, I wish above all things that thou mayest prosper and be in health, even as thy soul prospereth.

For I rejoiced greatly, when the brethren came and testified of the truth that is in thee, even as thou walkest in the truth."

—3 JOHN 2-3

"He openeth also their ear to discipline, and commandeth that they return from iniquity.

If they obey and serve him, they shall spend their days in prosperity, and their years in pleasures."

—JOB 36:10

And lastly, this most popular verse in the entire Bible:

"The LORD is my shepherd, I shall not want."

—PSALMS 23:1

WHOLESOME WELLNESS WITHIN YOUR CAMP

Re-visit with me, my opening scriptural verse in this chapter, would you, please? It reads:

"Let them shout for joy, and be glad, that favour my righteous cause: yea, let them say continually, Let the LORD be magnified, which hath pleasure in the prosperity of His servants."[1]

There are *two* key words in that instructive verse, above: *"favor"* and *"pleasure"*, the etymological roots of which we must have a firm grasp of, in order to be able to accurately arrive at their truest meanings!

Rendered in the original Hebrew tongue, both *"favor"* and *"pleasure"* synonymously translate the same: *"incline towards", "be pleased with", "desire", "delight"* and *"have pleasure in something or someone."*

According to *Collins Concise Dictionary*, to *"delight"* means *"to please greatly, take great pleasure in, have extreme pleasure in."*[2]

In other words, God has a great pleasure in the wellness, security and wholeness of your camps both *within* – and *without!*

When you bought – or were given the gift of a beautiful first wrist watch, for instance, you didn't shout "*Ma-na* –

What is this?" Rather, you immersed yourself in the gift's exquisite delicacy and finesse. You adored it!

Whenever I'd purchased *any* new gadget – if you were like me, you would examine it to its minutest details every so often, before laying it back in its protective wraps! You would rest a while, then again, repeat same feat, though I should confess, with a declining frequency! You're said to be *"delighting in"* the gift that has so enraptured you!

Why do you think it's any different with God?

Even though He makes *His* sun to shine upon all – and rain to fall upon the godly and the ungodly alike, the righteous and the unrighteous; yet there appears to be a thick line drawn upon the shores of eternity to differentiate those who *delight* themselves in Him *from* they who do not – or who just couldn't be bothered to!

But *if* you would observe to *delight* yourself in God, you would soon notice that He too would reciprocate your kind gesture with a special *delight* in you!

Now, *His* delight in *you* is superlatively incomparable to *your* delight in *your* new gift or toy – a *delight* which soon wears *thin* with time. No, God's delight in you will outlast time itself – because it simply is everlasting! This translates, if you were to be passing through 'Marah-land' just like Moses had with the children of Israel, God would more than delight in the minutest details of your sojourn and pain. His loving heart would be more than gladdened to show you how to turn the bitterness into sweetness, the mess into a message, the pain into 'pay-streams' – and heal *not* only your waters, but even your diseases, ailments and infirmities!

'Is all well within your camp?' my friend, may I ask!

I pray today that the Holy Spirit will quicken your *spirit* so as to begin to learn how to *delight* yourself in the God of your salvation.

There is a whole chunky lot more to your current status in life, than meets the eye! Most of life's battles – if not all – are fought in the *mind*. Your *mind* is the connection point between the spiritual and the physical worlds. It is also the battleground of the spirit-realm! It was in the *spirit* realm that physical things were first birthed and formed, before they eventually, finally, physically appeared in *our* world!

Oh, yes; there is a *spirit-realm* – which if I may be honest with you, is more real than the *physical* into which you automatically discovered yourself dispatched. You were delivered into – and have developed your physical senses here on earth; but actually, your *authentic specie* was fabricated after God's kind of being!

It is through this spiritual realm of existence that God's Holy Spirit could gain access into a man's *spirit* – and make him/her a totally new being that could influence the world with the help of a great deal of God's anointing, grace and favor! You see, God passionately requests available men and women who would mindfully yield and surrender unto Him to be used for His glory, here in this physical, *earthly* realm!

But humankind's arch-enemy, Satan, is *not* relenting. He competes roughly and unfairly to gain access to this vital component – the authentic man; the *spirit* of a man or woman! He achieves this feat primarily, through *fear*! He would mercilessly bombard any mind availed onto him and his demons through sinister scare-tactics. His battle-plan for gaining entry into and the possession of humans, again, are un-gentlemanly; *very* rough, ferocious, vicious – and calculatedly mean!

If anyone would avail the diabolical forces as little as an inch of their mind's land-space, they would invade such a mind and inevitably cause such unsuspecting landowners to forfeit, forcefully, a mile of their domain to wicked spirit-beings that engender wickedness, afflictions, wreckages and bondages on an immeasurably great magnitude! Therefore, it would seem agreeable to a keen mind to arrive at a very reasonable conclusion that *both* God and the devil desire to "possess" the human spirit – which in some cases may lead to a struggle, somewhat, depending upon *who* they yield unto!

Yielding unto the former leads to peace and fulfillment; the latter, turmoil, struggles and utter destruction!

'But why should humans be involved in their battle-engagement, anyway?', you ask!

The answer is pretty simple. Humans are involved in this ageless conflict because they are the only specie of being that is essentially *spirit* – who yet possesses visible, tangible bodies! We are fully *spirit-beings* encased in a strait-jacket called the *body*, with the *mind* well fitted somewhere between our *body* and *spirit*. We were essentially created by the Creator to *rejoice* and *delight* ourselves in the Him, alone! That specie of being that fails to delight itself in God is surely on a concocted sleeping pill administered by that forceful, un-gentlemanly, arch-rival, arch-enemy called Satan!

WHEN THE CHIPS ARE DOWN

"But while men slept, his enemy came and sowed tares among the wheat, and went his way."

— MATTHEW 13:25

Job done!

Re-read Jesus' statement above – and discover Satan's *modus operandi* in his field of expertise! Perversion sown; wild oat harvest-rewards, earnestly awaited!

When a *spirit-being* loses his mooring – God; all kinds of weird, demonic interferences and manifestations shall begin to fester in *all* realms of existence and experience. This is the 'struggle' I earlier mentioned! A person who *had* been well aligned with God for so many years soon gradually, for example, begins to wane in their desires to pursue *intimacy* and *delight* with their first Love. One proven, effective strategy of the spiritually diabolical world, over the centuries, is to pile up untold pressures of incalculable degree upon the mind of such persons *subdued under their influence*. The wicked one – Satan – and his demonic hosts will machinate every intrigue and attacking plot in their black books against such *'people of interest'* in order that they may continually be suppressed under their destructive demonic influences.

WHOLESOME WELLNESS WITHIN YOUR CAMP

Such influences ensure that their subjects *never* accurately receive the truest motions; neither sense the urgency in the things of the Spirit – or the *spiritual*. In other words they accurately ensure dulled spiritual senses! These wicked beings achieve their dare-devil feat by ensuring you spend more and more time away from a rejuvenating personal time with the Lord and His Word! That way, your core being – your *spirit* – would be reduced to a pitiable, weakened state of existence; you *"would become as weak as anyone else"*, according to backslidden Samson's proven observation![3]

Subjects *under the influence* of hell are kept from hungering and thirsting after God; the devils whisper into their ears to "just have an easy ride", "take it softly easy" or "just coast along". They gently and insidiously start drifting – like an unwary, napping, holidaying sun-bather on a raft at the edge of the shore who suddenly awoke to find him/herself in torrid ocean currents!

Are you – or someone you know, operating 'under the influence'; such unholy influence as described above?

Because Satan – and his mean co-hosts are masterly artisans in the business of cajoling, luring and stealthily stealing away, carefree souls. God's word however apportions *you* that sole responsibility of safe-keeping your *spirit*, that the wicked one poach you not.[4] If Satan succeeded in poaching you off your roots, his ultimate goal would be to kill and destroy *your* soul![5]

This is *the* root cause for all 'downed' *chips* in life!

But God wants it well with you!

He wants it *totally well* within your camp! More, He wants it *exemplarily well* with you – with every fiber in your muscle, every cell in your body, even unto the very notes in your pocketbook, wallet and purses! God wants it *absolutely well* with your health. Socially, He longs to see you well settled in your friendships and relationships – and above all else, spiritually; in your *delight* in Him alone.

And I pray for you: *"May it indeed be totally well with you in the name of the LORD!"*

3

WHEN THE CHIPS COME DOWN

Every bald eagle molts *at least* once in their average, thirty-year life span. The molting season is usually, a mournful, painful period of time for the big bird! No bald eagle prefers it, for it could last up to half a year – our *earth* year!

Molting is the process of the bald eagle's loss of his feathers starting first, from his head, down to every part of his plumage until he becomes bare and stark naked. At the end, he would have lost all of his tuft and plumes – his glory. (I know that some middle-aged man may be experiencing some 'tuft-loss', particularly at their crown, and thinking: *Oh, that sounds like me!* Oh, no; your gradual hair loss is in *no* way comparable to the bald eagle's molting experience).

Once this excruciating nature's season has fully set in, the once-majestic bird now bare, becomes vulnerable in many ways. He is also overtaken by an inexplicable psychological behavior, which, as a consequence causes him to droop his head. The calcium build-up on his beak not only makes his head a much heavier burden to lift and sustain in an upright position, but the eagle cannot even hunt for salmon, his favorite traditional meal!

Inarguably, this half-year dark omen doesn't in any way look attractive, nor is it least desiring. The once confident bird is now sad, mournful, depressed – and lonesome! The only panacea to his loneliness is his finding for company and comfort, other eagles who are undergoing the same experience, deep in the depth of the valley! And yes, down in that depth, he would have at least one more crucial need on his mind all day long: finding food supplies!

Apparently, due to his inability to hunt salmons, he may scavenge on other animals much weaker than him – and beneath him in his food chain! Because of *the* lack of a steady source of food supplies, a large number of such companies of naked birds will starve and perish. But the stronger ones also will eventually turn upon the weaker; pecking, wounding – and in most cases killing them, to satiate their hard-pinching hunger pangs! Survivability down there 'in the valley' becomes a tale of 'the survival of the fittest'.

However, despite the prevalent predatory lifestyle coupled with the existing hardships, there still exists a rare exemption to the unfortunate predicament of the bald eagles' *status quo*. These "rare exempt's" know by intuition that the *'valley'* atmosphere usually is crowded with as many different species as there are, trying to co-habit a restrictive territory by mutual, unspoken understanding! They thus refuse to endorse the understatement of congeniality in the comfort zone! These also refuse to prey – or indeed be preyed upon. Instead, they trade the common *survival mentality* for an *adventurous mentality!*

So instead of settling in on the *lee* in the valley, they begin an epic journey that is lonelier – and more precariously dangerous. These ones would pay any price to *not* stifle the adventurous spirit of their specie! Step by step – in beleaguered breathing accompanied by heavy, cumbersome stepping, each embarks upon the arduous climb.

WHEN THE CHIPS ARE DOWN

He perseveres.

He Endures.

He Rests.

He then resumes same cycle, only glancing once in a while at the summit upon which he has fixated his mind.

Once he arrives at the top of the crag, he is at liberty to now 'holiday'.

Soon, few other survivors too, begin to surface at the top!

These, indeed, are the *intuitive survivors*!

They lay in the open all day, in the sun's pathway for warmth; and much more – the highly expected meat *drop-offs* by possibly other older eagles which also had triumphed over their gruesome molting experiences!

The prophets Elijah, Jeremiah and John the Baptist were three well-known, chronic, Bible *eagle* characters whose *chips came down* not just often, but dare I say, very frequently! Their melancholic moments were explicitly, glaringly recorded for all to read! Yet, they were God's anointed servants!

WHEN THE CHIPS COME DOWN

David was the beloved king of Israel, but he had *had* quite many a time when things had gone rough *with* him – possibly also, due in part, to his own doings and/or un-doings.

Now, my quest for understanding still looms at variance:

- *Why should it surprise you if an anointed person fails morally or spiritually?*

- *Why have 'religious' people kept ministers of God on such a high pedestal of perfectionist trait – accorded by such so high, almost impossible-to-maintain expectations?*

- *Why do church 'followers'* – I didn't say Christ's followers – *get despondent, disillusioned, diverted, divisive and embittered if their leaders erred or failed?*

In my attempt to answer the questions above, permit me to categorically state:

Firstly, if you had 'root-depth' in spiritual matters and are *not* a spiritual 'babe' – for that is how scripture portrays those who are have *not* depths, you would realize that *your* faith should *not* be uprooted off from the depths of the knowledge and love of Christ *if* your man/woman of God fails or 'falls' short, in a potential area of their lives.[1]

Do not misunderstand me. This is *not* designed to sound as if I am advocating institutionalizing a preconceived *'margin of error'* rule here; neither am I placing your minister who has experienced a moral failure at your mercy to deal with as you would – or actually had wished! Either case would be tantamount to heretical teaching! Rather, I am aspiring to re-emphasize He in Whom *your* sum-total faith *should* rest!

> *"That your faith should not stand in the wisdom of men, but in the power of God."*[2]

Secondly, Spirit-filled people do *not* place ministers of God on *'celebrity status'* listing as does *Hollywood*. True, followers of Christ should definitely be well taught to accord respect to God's spiritual authorities, here on earth, no doubts. The dangerous shift of allegiance from the Lord onto another – a deadly infringement upon and an eroding of the bedrock of *spiritual babes'* faith – begins when a spiritual leader warms up to either the idea or actuality of being 'worshipped' by his parishioners or followers. Such a leader who condones or encourages this practice has desecrated that which belongs only, to the Divine God!

Men and women anointed of God – are ordinary, mere men, in the practical sense of being. The *nitty gritty* of daily living alone, proves that fact! (I know some religious big-wigs may not appreciate my re-affirming such truth since they would rather have you kept in the dark, anyway. See, you'd been 'brain-bleached' – since they'd always had you under a humanistic control; a form of subtlety and witchcraft). But the undeniable bottom-line truth remains that anointed people of God are *not* different to you!

Ministers of the gospel – and leaders battle the same thoughts and feelings that you, "the led", do battle against. They are tempted just like you are – and possibly, only more ferociously!

Sometimes, their marriages too hit the rocks and flail. Some actually do fail – in most cases, very fatally and most acrimoniously! Gomer, Prophet Hosea's wife played the whore to the core on numerous occasions despite the prophet's outnumbering attempts to restore her to himself![3] The earliest biblical writer – Job's wife had left him when things had gone sour for him![4] It is doubtless grave, when ills like these befall anointed, chosen persons of God; nevertheless, *they* do happen!

It is even much more grave when "upright" brothers and sisters who are meant to help support the "frail" and the "fallen" had actually looked down upon – and trampled upon them with no remorse, let alone any respect! Yet, these are 'broken' vessels who need healing – *not* castigation and/or despise!

When that ugly, despicable spirit of religious pride creeps into your mind to cause you to despise or abuse a "hero on zero", please beware! Pause – and have a second thought. In all honesty, that second thought might just as well lead you onto holding tight the reins of your tongue and having your steel gaze relaxed whilst you say a "silent prayer" for them!

Some of current day's ministers who had come out of addictive sinful lifestyles unto Christ, may still be heavily 'rocked' by the lure to the brutal savagery of their sinful past. Triumphantly though, a few who had emerged from such *'twisted'* backgrounds continue with huge *delight* in God's saving grace, serving Him ever so triumphantly. That's the way the Author of salvation intended it to be! However, *not* every such scion has had a safe, successful grafting though, onto the Vine – probably *not* un-attributable to its self-destructive undoing(s).

Similarly, almost in the same vein, *not* every minister or leader in God's vineyard overcomes the depressive, frustrating, lack-luster, 'burn-out' feelings that may – without prior warnings, plague leadership! As if bent on accomplishing an assignment from hell, a *'feedership'* congregation/followership then mounts such an odious pressure upon those leaders, to by every means become in public what they really are *not*, in private! This spiritually reckless attitude had always courted – and will continue to cause – the shipwreck of both a reckless leader and many an unstable soul!

Thirdly, a less-spiritual followership gets angry, disappointed, disillusioned and crushed in the 'spirit of their minds' when a leader they have 'up-scaled' higher than the Most High fails because of the spirit we humans are made of! We *were* made perfect, after the order of *the* Perfect Creator – the Most High God! Hence, there's an insatiable quest in us that tends to both expect and possibly request an almost 'perfectionist' touch from others!

But why would you allow yourself to be crushed 'in the spirit of your mind' if a leader fails to meet your abnormal expectations, when your very spirit has such an unrestricted, great, ample, opportunity to rather connect directly with the Divine, Most High God?

Based upon the afore-mentioned premises, you would agree with me that *no* one may be said to be completely exempt from encountering life's tough challenges!

Contrary to what you have been taught by the religion and tradition of men, God's ministers too are by no means exempt from encountering stiff, gigantic challenges – even in their walks with the Lord! In all honesty, they have actually always ranked "highest priority" on the devil's "*WANTED*" list!

The phrase *"when the chips are down"*, therefore, is an idiomatic expression often used to describe moments of huge discouragement and disconcertion of the soul brought about by extraneous circumstances that could take any – or a combination of these forms: physical, fiscal, social, psycho-emotional and/or spiritual.

Moments *"when the chips are down"* could also be referred to as "down times"; such times as when the state of affairs of an entity dwells in critical, rock-bottom, tough and dangerous *doldrums* – just as the once majestic bald eagle, now inhabiting his painful *'valley of molting'*!

No Exempt, Free Pass!

We, just like the great bald eagle, may do well to be reassured of experiencing – at least – *a* molting experience in our lifetime! Our individual reactions however to adversity are greatly consequential, reverberating onto our eternal tapestry's fabric!

Surprisingly, while no one may be fully guaranteed an 'exempt pass' from tough times, different people – and indeed different nations of the world have been known to have undergone "critical times" in their respective histories, yet had emerged victorious! Like the surviving bald eagles emerging from their molting experiences, these ones had emerged triumphant with iron, forged at the very core of their souls, having been submerged in troubles – and raised up wiser, stronger and ready to lay claims upon conquering higher heights and deeper depths!

A 'broken' eagle which survives the gruesome, harrowing molting experience emerges as an embodiment of stark beauty!

It re-emerges *re-birthed* and *renewed!*

Factually, it 'shows up' having grown longer, stronger feathers which could span a tip-to-tip width measurement of 6.5 feet in males and 7.5 feet in females. This graceful creature would also have developed new features such as sharper talons and beaks; its curved new beak, rated as sharp as a surgeon's scalpel!

This triumphant creature is analogous of Isaiah's prophecy in the forty-first chapter of his book, meant for anyone whom you might kindly and considerably judge as currently undergoing an unpleasant *'valley of molting'* experience:

> *"Fear not, thou worm Jacob, and ye men of Israel; I will help thee, saith the LORD, and thy redeemer, the Holy One of Israel.*
>
> *Behold, I will make thee a new sharp threshing instrument having teeth ..."*

—Isaiah 41:14-15

The 'molted' eagle, contrary to one of the Native Americans' superstitious beliefs, never re-incarnates. It has only *re-modeled* into a newer, stronger creature; more developed with wisdom, compassion and understanding. That's the Creator's mandate to the bald eagle. Same as it is to *you* in particular, who currently abide in the 'shadows'; in the *very* depths of '*the valley*'!

Let no spiritualist or religious pundit sweet-talk your mind persuasively away from the certainty of the existence of such excruciating times when your faith *will* be sore tried. Your faith will be tried *not* essentially because you've sinned against the Lord; it is rather justly, the way life here on earth had evolved ever since the *wicked one* – the devil, the dragon – had come to pitch tents with mankind, following his expulsion from Heaven!⁵

But he keeps fighting a long lost battle; he never learns!

This battle with the dragon the Bible re-assuredly explains to God's saints as the *"trial of your faith."*⁶

Accepting Jesus Christ as Savior and Lord will *not* automatically absolve you from encountering trying times or the bitter *waters of Marah*. I know you're bewildered to read that, but it nonetheless is the truth. Rather, what your decision to *"follow Jesus Christ no matter the cost"* avails you, is infuse your *within* – your spirit being – with the very strength of the Divine God, alongside the everlasting re-assurances of His Divine presence, *without*.

The Lord Jesus Christ would never contract out your *spirit-man* to 'Complacency-land.' Instead, He would always motion and beckon His followers to aspire and *"Come up hither."*⁷

This Savior, may I inform your hearing, has *never* been – and will never be – satisfied with that follower, toting and following Him from afar-off; he/she will necessarily need to close ranks. Neither is He pleased with *that* one who probably has plateaued and settled for the dregs of existential living – dragging, barely surviving and getting by; he/she too will be requested to shed and lay aside *"every weight which so easily weighs them down – so that they may run with patience that heaven-bound race, set before them!"*[8]

The Creator of the universe didn't create your *spirit* to be content occupying the various "comfort zones" of life. You are too 'loaded' for that!

Comfort zones are nothing but plateaus of dregs of subsistence, barely getting by!

You have plateaued in your spiritual walk once you have started to think and act out of alignment with God's Word.

You have compromised your specie's specifications once you wouldn't open your mouth to declare what God had already declared about you: *shut mouths, shut destinies!*

You have started spreading your tents in the *'valley of despair'* once you have started *not* fulfilling your vows, made before the Lord!

WHEN THE CHIPS COME DOWN

You have compromised the saving grace of the Lord Jesus Christ when you have started getting shy and 'slowing down' witnessing unto others about Him!

Are you plateaued in mediocrity – stationed on the dregs of subsistence, barely getting by?

His true followers, their hearts' love, He kindles!

His obedient followers, their fire for service, He stokes!

His call to His swooping battalion, again, is *"Come up hither!"*

"Come up hither", unto new heights of revelation that He alone gives in moments of alone.

"Come up hither", unto new depths of the riches and wisdom of God.

"Come up hither", unto a gentler, kindler, more compassionate *you* awaiting discovery and super-connection with the Divine!

Scripture teaches that God, in bringing many sons unto glory, made Jesus Christ the *"Captain of their salvation perfect through suffering."*[9] As their Redeemer-Captain, He does guarantee them resounding victories in the face of life's tests, sorrows, disappointments and heartaches – because He had *had* a first-rate, un-paralleled experience of whatever they may now encounter!

Do you know Jesus Christ as the Captain of your soul's salvation?

As *the* Captain, He Himself had been sore tried, yet He had emerged triumphant and victorious.[10] Because of His valiant strength, He succors with unlimited grace, *anyone* undergoing the nerve-racking experience of unjust trials and the stiffest oppositions! Listen to His re-assuring words:

> *"These things I have spoken unto you, that in me ye might have peace. In the world ye shall have tribulations: but be of good cheer; I have overcome the world."*
>
> —JOHN 16:33

Christian persecutions, trials and temptations are an integral side of *the* equation; the other equally important component side, folk may find hard to accept is the truth that people too often hit the hard, rock-bottom, *not* primarily essentially because of the trial of their faith, *but* because of their foolhardiness and un-informed poor choices, such as had done, the rebellious Jerusalem of Jeremiah's days.

When Judah's Chips Came Down

The nation of Israel – comprising of the ten northern tribes – had been obliterated due to their abominable sinful practices. They had decamped from following the Lord God Who had brought them *"out of the land of Egypt, out of the house of bondage"* through years of subscribing to the basest of choices and decisions![11] They had followed hard-nosed, on the restored worship of Ashtoreth, Baal – and other wretched, accursed gods of the lands God had once through them, conquered!

Quite insane, isn't it?

The nation of Judah – comprising of the two southern tribes of Benjamin and Judah – also had towed the destructive pathways that had led to her brother, Israel's full extinction. Had it not been for God's ir-revocable covenant with Abraham passed onto David, the Kingdom of Judah would never have returned from the Babylonian exile – which for record purposes had spanned seventy years!

Her capital city, Jerusalem had finally fallen to the brutal, savage blows and burning dealt it by the ruthless Babylonians' third and final massive raid in 586BC –

following their earlier raids of 605BC and 597BC, respectively!

There had been earlier failed capture attempts by several other uncouth, uncultured nations as Assyria and Syria – to name just two; these nations had over the years, weakened her defenses! Suddenly, at the feet of the brutal Babylonian soldiers, all of Judah's *chips* had come to rest on bare ground! It had been two decades that prophet Jeremiah had first forewarned of this calamitous day; alas it had come upon her – and her unrepentant, rebellious, stiff-necked citizens!

There comes a time in *a* person's, *a* people's – or *a* nation's history when they must own up and recognize the reasons for sustaining such losses and ravages of wars, diseases and epidemics! The culture of "Blame the Top" ought to cease! An intuitive bald eagle that will re-emerge stronger, must own responsibility for the precarious journey from the *'valley'* onto the *mountain-top* where he receives supplies, by faith alone! He also neither blames anyone for his molting experience. Rather, he decodes his experience as nature's challenge to him to: *"Come – develop and grow new pair of stronger wings so as to be able to conquer greater heights, above greater storms!"*

WHEN THE CHIPS COME DOWN

This wise creature sees this unpleasant season of molting, as an opportunity to modify, renew, re-define and re-emerge; the whole sustained pain is *not* a consequence of a self-inflicted wound!

When you have consumed so much soda and 'fizzy-pops' over the years, for instance – and now a decade later are diagnosed with a wasting internal disease, you shouldn't get bitter and angry. Rather, that diagnosis should serve you a 'wake-up call' to either modify or re-define your intake of sugary and carbonated water. A good dietician following his prognostic mind would request that you be placed on a strict regimen of healthy diet alternatives, drinking ordinary water and observing 'sweaty' exercise schedules, for the rest of your days. Then, you *should* soon begin to observe a re-defined, healthier you, re-emerging!

That's how best it sounds!

Only a few people however, would be realistic enough to own responsibility for their poor dietary and drinking habits – plus lack of exercise as the root-causes to an ill-health. Most would find it much easier diligently searching for an excuse to proffer; someone or *some* circumstance to blame – not forgetting the precious *few* that will readily blame *genetics!*

WHEN THE CHIPS ARE DOWN

Judah – like many on a self-inflicted destructive pathway – had *not* accepted responsibility for her wounds and afflictions. Both her kings and priests had lived a lie. The prophet Jeremiah, however – along with his secretary, Baruch and one or two other city-dwellers had been exceptions to their compatriots' lifestyles *living* – and *leading a lie*.

Jeremiah had expounded prophetically to the inhabitants of Judah and Jerusalem for forty years, God's intent of punishing Jerusalem, their beloved city and the captivity of Judah through super-power Babylon without recording a native resident penitent soul!

He hadn't been only a *mouthpiece of God* – but also a *living witness* to the price anyone should be willing to pay for defying the Almighty God! He literally had portrayed Judah's disposition when her feathers had been plucked by Babylon – and her *chips*, rested!

As he had castigated the king, his noblemen, the lawmakers and Judah's rebellious ways, the *living witness* had consequentially been arrested, beaten and jailed repeatedly, having escaped official execution by God's favor, alone! (Read his interesting book and learn for yourself what it means to 'have a spine', you spineless *'feedership'* follower of the Way! You will likely become emotional and weep bitterly for your casual, wayward ways!)

Both in *private* and in *public*, the prophet had witnessed the evils in Judah, firsthand: the hunger and the starvation, the horrendous massacre of the citizenry and young children on the streets of Jerusalem, the emotionally traumatic abduction of children away from families in chariot-loads by the invading captors and the final reduction of the ancient city to ashes!

Maybe you too are living a lie, today!

Perhaps, you've fallen for the enemy's propaganda regarding your life and destiny. You've possibly settled for a life of mediocrity! Probably you don't even know that *your* "chips are down"; *'After all, many other birds haven't even got any wings'*, you brag!

Take a glance, at Prophet Jeremiah's vivid portrait of a people *whose chips were down*, in his poetic account:

> *"Jerusalem's streets, once bustling with people, are now silent. Like a widow broken with grief, she sits alone in her mourning. Once the queen of the nations, she is now a slave.*

WHEN THE CHIPS ARE DOWN

She sobs through the night; tears stream down her cheeks. Among all her lovers, there is no one left to help her. All her friends have betrayed her; they are now her enemies."

Do those descriptions befit you – or someone you know?

Read some more:

"Judah has been led away into captivity, afflicted and enslaved. She lives among foreign nations and has no place of rest. Her enemies have chased her down, and she has nowhere to turn.

The roads to Jerusalem are in mourning, no longer filled with crowds on their way to celebrate the Temple festivals. The city gates are silent, her priests groan, her young women are crying – how bitterly Jerusalem weeps!

Her oppressors have become her masters, and her enemies prosper, for the LORD has punished Jerusalem for her many sins. Her children have been captured and taken away to distant lands.

All the beauty and majesty of Jerusalem are gone. Her princes are like starving deer searching for pasture, too weak to run from the pursuing enemy.

WHEN THE CHIPS COME DOWN

And now in the midst of her sadness and wandering, Jerusalem remembers her ancient splendor. But then she fell to her enemy, and there was no one to help her. Her enemy struck her down and laughed as she fell.

Jerusalem has sinned greatly, so she has been tossed away like a filthy rag. All who once honored her now despise her, for they have seen her stripped naked and humiliated. All she can do is groan and hide her face.

She defiled herself with immorality with no thought of the punishment that would follow. Now she lies in the gutter with no one to lift her out. 'LORD, see my deep misery,' she cries, 'The enemy has triumphed.'

Her people groan as they search for bread. They have sold their treasures for food to stay alive. 'O LORD, look,' she mourns, 'and see how I am despised.'"

—LAMENTATIONS 1:1-10 & 11;
NLT, Life Application Study Bible Version

Sin against the Lord should bring *any* person, community or nation down – and out! Listen to King Solomon aptly say it:

"Righteousness exalteth a nation: but sin is a reproach to any people."

—PROVERBS 14:34

In pre-historic times, there had been an *'escape goat'* – from which was derived the term 'scape-goat'! This goat, *a* sin-bearer, was that upon which the high priest had laid his hands and confessed the entire sins of the whole nation before leading him out of town and releasing him into the wilderness to die.

Now, that goat was symbolic of Jesus, our Paschal Lamb – and *the* eternal Sin-bearer of the whole world! He had been crucified and raised again for an eternal remission – taking away – of the sins of the whole world. By His redeeming power am I sent this day, to proclaim unto you this everlasting truth: whatever factor lays at the root of your suffering, trials and shame; whether it be as a result of your enduring faith starring the devil in the eye, or as the consequence of that foolish act you have conducted or condoned, *the eternal sacrifice of God's Lamb has cut the deal; He shall ransom you, re-emerge you wiser, stronger, cleansed and better-equipped than before you approached the dark haze!*

You may have no courage to want to get up out of bed – and face the challenges of a bright new day. You'd rather prefer to stay under the duvet or coverlet for fears of impending harm or hurt! Could well be that your undesirable lifestyle had been forced upon you – arising as result of a heavy bout of depression or ill-health!

WHEN THE CHIPS COME DOWN

Probably, the doctors have delivered you *the* dreaded news. Or your bank loan department's number has just been displayed on your receiving device's screen – but you couldn't dare take their call; your heart is pounding so heavily against its rib-cage. Possibly, your mortgage arrears have slipped into the red strip zone called "missed payments" for a disengaging consecutive past five months – and you're about to be foreclosed upon!

Your refrigerator may be empty – with young children whining for food despite your job loss in these extraordinarily challenging times; remember each of those children reserve the exclusive rights to expect you to conjure food on the table anyway – and possibly anyhow!

How would you, then, explain the recessionary trends to a hungry child?

Listen, dear friend, the miraculous Jesus Christ, Son of the living God, is able to bear you through – and re-emerge you from the *'valley of lowliness'* and the belly of affliction, stronger and wiser than prior your *'chips being down'*! Only one requirement would be helpful: your ability to lift up your voice and dial Heaven's hotline. God's forever promise is if/when we call on Him, He will answer – and disclose unto us deep secrets hitherto unknown:

WHEN THE CHIPS ARE DOWN

"Call unto me, and I will answer thee, and shew thee great and mighty things, which thou knowest not."

—JEREMIAH 33:3

4

FOUR PROVEN, LIFE-SUSTENANCE PRINCIPLES

Thus far, I have attempted to awaken your awareness to the absolute truth that God wants it well – in fact, *very* well, both *'within'* and *'without'* your camps. Additionally, I have endeavored to portray the idiomatic expression *"When the chips are down"* through my depiction of the painful experiences a molting bald eagle endures whilst undergoing a molting season!

Now, whilst you steadfastly entrust the Lord with *your* general welfare and safe-keep, it will interest you to note that the Lord too, has implicitly faithfully entrusted you with, both, the *safe-keep* and *upkeep* of other eagle-beings that may have fallen prey to the various caprices of *'the fowler'* – the devil.[1] Therefore, it will serve both a great deal of generosity – on your part – and an awakening to duty, to be enamored with sufficient truth that ought to be applied in order to rescue self – or indeed, *another*, sinking in the quicksand of trying times. This is my objective in this chapter: to equip you like a fire-rescuer; ready to embark on a rescue mission, wherever, *if* ever, duty beckons!

Based on the thought-provoking journal entries of the afflicted Prophet Jeremiah, you will rescue – and/or become rescued from the *'valley of molting'*, if you *would* engage these *four* spiritual principles:

- Recalling the Lord's mercies in peace times
- Keeping alive your hope in Him alone
- Waiting for the Lord's rescue plan, and finally;
- Faithfully engaging in the character-development exercise He has enrolled you in.

Jeremiah's Four Proven, Life-sustenance Principles in the 'Valley of Molting'

Now, shall we evaluate each of these spiritually dynamic life-sustaining principles, more closely?

FOUR PROVEN, LIFE-SUSTENANCE PRINCIPLES

1. *Remember to Re-call the Lord's Mercies*

"This I recall to my mind, therefore I have hope.

It is of the Lord's mercies that we are not consumed, because His compassions fail not."

—LAMENTATIONS 3:21-22

This is the wisest, easiest thing to do: *recall the Lord's mercies* every blessed day you awake! Developing, cultivating and practicing this healthy habit *should* keep you out of plenty trouble!

Now, in case you are already *in* trouble, you must endeavor to recall to your mind, the Lord's mercies in particular, *before* your advent into sojourning in the *'valley'*!

Some, obviously, are *not* that wise, are they?

Many more are so ungrateful to the extent that they trivialize even the very littlest acts of grace, mercy and kindness of the past, received of the Lord.

Unwise souls arrogate God's mercies and kindness as mere *'essentials'*; they regard them as their legal, legitimate entitlements. Then they get into trouble, and – *voila*; the eyes of their minds become even more beclouded by the 'dizzy spells' caused by the unexpected turn of events in the low tides of life!

Their 'low-tide' could be a jailhouse, an unexpected bad news or a sudden job lay-off! For some still, theirs is a 'hook' on the roulette wheel or gambling machine suddenly registering a five-figure-sum-loss in blinking, fleeting seconds!

You would be deemed 'the wisest being on the earth' now, if you would commence *recalling the Lord's mercies of past years*, in the very midst of your turmoil. Both *His* 'big' acts – and *His* 'little' deeds!

Start with such a thought of gratitude as this:

> *His redemption of me was invaluable; yet, He had paid the full price! He'd ransomed me by the atoning sacrificial death of Jesus Christ, the Righteous!*

If you've never experienced God's saving grace, I may be persuaded to understand your rationale of questioning *recalling the Lord's mercies*. (I shall be addressing you more specifically in *Chapter 5*). However, *if* you indeed, are a beneficiary of God's gift of eternal salvation, you should *never* trivialize His act of ir-reconcilable grace!

FOUR PROVEN, LIFE-SUSTENANCE PRINCIPLES

Start your day, therefore, thanking Him for saving your soul from eternal hell fire!

Recall; you, who were *"dead in trespasses and sins; wherein in time past ye walked according to the courses of this world, according to the prince of the power of the air, the spirit that now worketh in the children of disobedience."*[2]

Recall God's mercy and grace that delivered you from the *snare of the fowler* – saved, sanctified and restored!

Recall Jesus' everlasting once-for-all sacrifice upon the cross on Golgotha's hill vis-à-vis His suffering, death and taking your judgment and hell so that you wouldn't ever have to stand before *Heaven's Criminal Justice Court!*

You may *not* fully understand the implications of Jesus' *Finished Work* if you never had a reason to stand before a magistrate or judge!

I once had that privilege! A 'royal invitation' had been extended to me by mail – an invitation on behalf of Her Royal Majesty – to stand before a Magistrate in 2006 after the Police had summoned me on a Motor Traffic related offence. In the end, I had represented myself – and had bagged three points on my driver's license with an additional monetary fine which had been in the vicinity of lesser than a hundred *odd* pounds, the exact amount of which I cannot recall at present! Come to think of the apprehensive tension that had pervaded my world before the hearing date; I could only confess – in retrospect – that those weeks had been the most agonizingly excruciating weeks I'd ever witnessed!

That lone incident was the *one* single less-careful, splashed-over stroke of *the law's* sash brush on my life's canvas painting, in my entire life. But I had *had* an eternal summons dangling, loosely over my head; a case which I would have been left with no other option but plead *"Guilty!"* That would surely have earned me a sentence to eternal damnation! The baseline had changed when I had accepted Christ's redemptive sacrifice on the Cross. That had been His gift to *me* – my acceptance of which had made *His Gift* become personally, *mine!* This salvation gift package is in-exchangeable; in other words, it is non-negotiable!

Not only had Jesus pled *"Guilty"* on your behalf and been eternally sentenced to the maximum punishment for your sins, too – He'd kept delivering you from all evils. Recall His past deliverances over your life: physical, soulish, material, financial – and otherwise!

FOUR PROVEN, LIFE-SUSTENANCE PRINCIPLES

More, recall *all* He'd since been through *with* you – always by your side. He hadn't left, forsaken or abandoned you in the heat of life's battles. Rather, He'd stayed true to you!

The prophet Jeremiah, for instance, had recalled in exact details, the rough scenarios pursuant to his release from prison before the eventual Babylonian captivity that had flattened Judah, good nineteen years after the first battalion's troops' boots had been set on Judah-land! He had vividly re-called how he had been thrown into Malchiah's deep dungeon to die of starvation via the instrumentation, plotting and scheming of the princes and the Council! He had been 'ditched' in that dungeon, but from an unlikely, unexpected source, God had raised him help, in an African – an Ethiopian eunuch by the name, Ebedmelech.[3]

Not only had the suffering prophet 'gained upon favor' from an unlikely slave-source, *favor* had widely smiled on him through the supposedly wicked, foreign invading-king Nebuchadrezzar – and Nebuzaradan, his captain of the guard whom he had specifically commanded concerning the prophet:

> *"Take him and look after him well. Do him no harm but deal with him as he may ask of you."*

> —JEREMIAH 39:12;
> Amplified Version

Thus, the servant of God had been well kept and looked after throughout the invasion and captivity of the exiles. He'd lived peacefully in Judah, among his own clan – until every word of prophesy he had proclaimed about Judah and Jerusalem had been fulfilled! (Even when he had been forcefully exiled to Egypt by *Johanan & Co.*, God's presence had *never* departed from him!)

The despised prophet, at last, had *gained upon favor!*

That surely sounds like you, too, *gaining upon favor* from every quarter, this season of your life – and for the rest of your days in the favorable name of Jesus Christ!

Whoa!

Think of it: favor *of* God, *from* God, *through* God; from both 'likely' and seemingly 'unlikely' sources, *surrounding, pursuing* – and *overtaking* you!

Glory to God!

This evidently pinpoints a basic, fundamental element in '*gaining upon God's favor*': God's favor is *not* relegated to a fixed depot! In other words, the favor of God upon an individual, a family, a community or a people *cannot* be restricted neither relegated! If ever a restriction/arrest

FOUR PROVEN, LIFE-SUSTENANCE PRINCIPLES

order was placed upon FAVOR, He would burst forth from *all* sides!

Joseph, like Jeremiah had escaped a heinous death plot. Rather than being slain, he had similarly been dumped in a deep pit. It may not have sounded like it but that was *favor* – right there and then in the pit with Joseph! Soon, same *favor* would rescue him out alive, for the next leg of his journey into destiny!

Here's an underscore of a tremendously important lesson: even when the situations of life had turned out to *not* be as exactly as you had thought they would have transpired, be thankful and optimistic – for *favor* had got you thus far, and neither is willing to part ways with you, ever!

Also, if the earth be shut tight, *favor* would burst forth, right from above the very skies, rendering the Heavens open! That had been Jesus' experience at His baptism in the very depth of *Jordan* – 'Jordan', the very depth of death! The eyes of His compatriots had been shut like blinkers on a horse, *but* the *very* Heavens had opened up upon Him and had accorded Him the respect mortal beings had blindly denied Him! He had forever been declared as God's very own pleasing Beloved Son by the voice of *neither* reason nor treason, but *Favor*, Personified!

WHEN THE CHIPS ARE DOWN

> *"For he received from God the Father honor and glory, when there came such a voice unto him from the excellent glory, This is my beloved Son, in whom I am well pleased."*

—2 PETER 1:17

May I boldly declare unto you this very moment that God has declared *you* too, His *very* beloved, with whom He is well pleased!

Stop selling yourself, short, therefore! You must at once earnestly begin expecting and positioning yourself for *your* Heavens which are about to be rent wide open above your head, even in the very belly of *your* 'Jordan' – or in the very of depths of *your* 'valley'!

As you do, keep in mind, though, to *not* be an ingrate – a vain recipient of God's mercies!

The handsome-faced, teenaged shepherd boy David, was a thousand and one miles clear of an ungrateful heart! He had deployed this principle I am expounding to you; *the principle of recalling the Lord's mercies* every day – and had been assured of multiple victories in spite of his many slips. Despite his numerous weaknesses, God's eyes had sought and had found Him *"a man after his own heart"* (1 Samuel 13:14). You must – by now –

FOUR PROVEN, LIFE-SUSTENANCE PRINCIPLES

know both *'how'* and *'why'* that could ever have been possible!

You see, winning God's Favor-heart is always ever possible if your heart be first, grateful, yet recognizing and acknowledging your inadequacies!

Favor delights in grateful hearts who through grateful lips can always recall God's mercies, all day long!

> *"Surely, goodness and mercies shall follow me all the days of my life: and I will dwell in the house of the LORD for ever."*

> —PSALMS 23:6

David had discovered the *'Gratitude Principle'* and had never for once failed to captivate God's heart and re-direct the focus of His merciful gaze unto the army of Israel, *"his prisoners of hope"* locked up in their strongholds of fear.[4]

Probably you too are a prisoner of hope, landlocked by fear?

I graciously ask that you be not spiritually ignorant of the mechanics of 'gaining upon' God's *favor* in your situation!

Handsome David, though young in physical age, had been deeply steeped and rooted in spiritual understanding!

WHEN THE CHIPS ARE DOWN

When he had been faced with the most formidable opposition of his 'recollect-ability': the Philistine champ Goliath, he had aptly re-called the "sure mercies of God" unto him whilst he had kept those few sheep in the desert!

He didn't just rush ahead to confront Goliath!

No; he'd first got together, his *battle-cry*!

There's a turn in the atmosphere, in favor of all those, who despite facing gigantic mountains of opposition, would *not* confront those humongous barriers in their own strength – nor with their technical proficiencies, but in the power of God's Holy Spirit!

Before the four-foot tall, reddish-complexioned thirteen year old would steer towards the ten-foot Philistine warrior, he'd *first* stirred up his battle-cry: *God's sure mercies*. He had re-called how he'd witnessed past, great, deliverances of the Lord away from the paws of the bear and the jaws of the lion that had, at different occasions attempted to snatch away a lamb from the fold – or had in fact posed a threat to *his* very own well-being!

> *"And David said unto Saul, Thy servant kept his father's sheep, and there came a lion, and a bear, and took a lamb out of the flock:*

FOUR PROVEN, LIFE-SUSTENANCE PRINCIPLES

And I went out after him, and smote him, and delivered it out of its mouth: and when he arose against me, I caught him by his beard, and smote him, and slew him.

Thy servant slew both the lion and the bear: and this uncircumcised Philistine shall be as one of them, seeing he hath defied the armies of the living God."

—1 Samuel 17:34-36

Wasn't *gratitude*, Jesus' *attitude* when he'd been faced with the dilemma of feeding the multitude? Wasn't it that He had *first* lifted those five loaves and two small fishes up to Heaven and had given thanks to His Heavenly Father for always hearing him before the supernatural had occurred?

"And when he had taken the five loaves and the two fishes, he looked up to heaven, and blessed, and brake the loaves, and gave them to his disciples to set before them; and the two fishes divided he among them all."

—Mark 6:41

'What is the correlation between lifting a young boy's packed lunch box into the sky, praying to an unseen God – and as a result, feeding 5 000 men with twelve basketful of remnants gathered, anyway?' you ask!

You're right! There's absolutely *no* correlation to the naked eye or the physical senses that should have guaranteed any miracle of multiplicity! But the Lord Jesus Christ was stirring His *battle-cry of gratitude* in order to be able to 'gain upon' His Father's *favor*! And He *sure* had! His demonstration was a precedent to us – that we too will never lose *whatever* battle we are engaged in *whenever* we have first stirred up within our spirit, the battle-cry of *recalling the mercies of the Lord*!

A man who had witnessed the salvation and deliverance of the Lord had written the lyrics of this song:

> *"Bless the LORD, O my soul: and all that is within me, bless his holy name.*
>
> *Bless the LORD, O my soul, and forget not all his benefits:*
>
> *Who forgiveth all thine iniquities; who healeth all thy diseases;*
>
> *Who redeemeth thy life from destruction; who crowneth thee with lovingkindness and tender mercies;*
>
> *Who satisfieth thy mouth with good things; so that thy youth is renewed like the eagle's."*[5]

FOUR PROVEN, LIFE-SUSTENANCE PRINCIPLES

2. *Remember to Keep Alive, your Hope in God Alone*

"The LORD is my portion, saith my soul; therefore will I hope in Him"

—LAMENTATIONS 3:24

Permit me to avail you this verse, in the *Amplified* version of the Bible, thus:

"The LORD is my portion or my share says my living being, my inner self, therefore will I hope in Him and wait expectantly for Him."

Bear in mind, the word *"share"* in the *Amplified* translation above, for I shall soon return to its importance in rendering us a fuller understanding of our discussion!

Now, when someone is said to *have* 'hope', it translates they *have* feelings of expectation, desire and confidence that what they desire will become reality!

Hope and *faith* are two separate entities!

While *faith* solely rests upon God's express will backed by an unfailing, guaranteed eagerness to perform or fulfill His Word; *hope* on the other hand depends entirely, upon *one* drawing out, with eager expectation, from that which he/she had first securely held in place.

True *'hope'* that Prophet Jeremiah was talking about in that verse quoted above subsists entirely upon *your* positive *co-relationship* with God. For instance, when you go to the bank to make a withdrawal, you present your card and account details to the cashier or bank official. You then authorize the transaction with your signature – thus now 'placing a demand', so to say, on that which you had *first held in place!*

Operating the same analogy above by *faith* is a completely different ball-game, however! This entails you visiting your bank branch armed with your banking details to withdraw an amount of money *a trusted other has expressly informed you, they have deposited in, on your behalf!* This transaction does *not* require you putting anything in safe-keep prior to you making that demand. Rather, you just 'show up' and stash cash, cashing in on *their* generosity!

If you understood the clarity between both concepts above, then, you may legally ask yourself: *'Could it ever be possible that I make a demand of a withdrawal on an account into which I have not made any savings?'*

FOUR PROVEN, LIFE-SUSTENANCE PRINCIPLES

The answer is obvious! *Yes, you could!*

You sure could, because, again, *a trusted other* may have deposited a fortune into your bank account, secretly, without your knowledge, as a pleasant game of catching you by a pleasant surprise! Lovers do it all the time – and I'm aware, that's the kind of surprise I wouldn't mind!

Now, their gesture of goodwill of a 'worthy' deposit automatically becomes your "share" – your worthy "portion" *if* you become knowledgeable of their loving benevolence. You *may* remain stark 'broke', however, if you are unaware of some good money just sitting in your bank account, awaiting your orders!

However, *if* you become knowledgeable of your "portion", you shouldn't ever have a problem with laying claim on it; it's already in *your* account, isn't it?

Now, have you any stake, portion or share in the Lord? Are you aware of it?

Many are *not* aware of their worthy share in God! If you are aware of the rich deposits the Lord holds in place for you however, this is one huge reason you are more than qualified to *not* fear a day 'when the chips are down'!

Rather, you should be emboldened to unreservedly lay claim on your secure, "worthy portion".

Take for instance, those faithful partners who help me further the work of the ministry by partnering – and sowing consistently their time, talents and treasures yearly, monthly, weekly and daily; the Lord of the harvest, Whom they have decided to principally partner with has expressly assured them that He will *not* forget their labor of love, come low or high tide. Doing so equates Him to being unrighteous! But we are re-assured by the scriptures, time and again, that He is a just and righteous God – the Worthiest Partner in *any* venture:

> *"For God is not unrighteous to forget your work and labour of love, which ye have shewed toward his name, in that ye have ministered to the saints, and do minister."*
>
> —HEBREWS 6:10

What a guaranteed assurance!

But wait; there is a further encouragement and admonition:

> *"And we desire that every one of you do shew the same diligence to the full assurance of hope unto the end."*
>
> —HEBREWS 6:11

FOUR PROVEN, LIFE-SUSTENANCE PRINCIPLES

In other words, *follow through* with a disciplined consistence, your 'living hope' in God that you had first laid hold upon as your Eternal, exceeding Great Reward! Don't you ever let anyone talk you out of your *hope* – your *stake*, your *worthy portion* and *share!*

Now, *if* trouble assails such a believer who has put their *total* hope in the Lord therefore, it would *not* be wrong for them to – in turn – put God in remembrance of *all* their investments in His holy cause(s).

"Put me in remembrance: let us plead together: declare thou, that thou mayest be justified" His word reminds us, through Prophet Isaiah![6]

"And call upon me in the day of trouble: I will deliver thee, and thou shalt glorify me", God – Who cannot lie – promises through the Psalmist.[7]

Remember Nehemiah's magnanimity toward the Lord?

He had become the Governor of Judah during the reconstruction of the wall of Jerusalem – a time of unprecedented hardship and financial unsettlement. But he had made an outstanding resolution which no leader before him had made: he had refused the salary apportionment due the 'Office of the Governor' not for a mere couple of months – but for *good* twelve years! And he hadn't taken a kick-back or a bribe, all that time! Think about that for a while – and think about yourself exchanging *shoes* with him!

> *"Now these were prepared for each day: one ox and six choice sheep; also fowls were prepared for me, and once in ten days a store of all sorts of wine. Yet for all this, I did not demand [my rights] the food allowed me as a governor, for the [tribute] bondage was heavy upon this people."*

—NEHEMIAH 5:18;
Amplified Version

So how had he and his family sustained themselves?

Ah, the answer to that is pretty an easy one, too: *the Gov.* had lived to see his *living, active, expectant hope in God,* fully realized!

For a man purposed to 'live by faith' alone, his supposedly fat salary had been "apportioned" unto becoming a burnt sacrifice unto God, the Possessor of Heaven and earth! This meant that Governor Nehemiah had deposited a "worthy portion, share or stake" in God's pot, practically speaking!

FOUR PROVEN, LIFE-SUSTENANCE PRINCIPLES

He had also possessed the knowledge that God had *never* – and *would never* be *any* person's Debtor but that He *does* repay with huge dividends, *everything* forgone for His cause or "potted" in His kitty![8]

Isn't that revelation worthy of consideration by potential investors and stakeholders searching for one genuine, worthy investment into which they could invest which also guarantees a hundred percent return – and more, an eternal yield?

You see, God – and God alone ought to be *your* main, primary Source upon Whom you expectantly hope!

This is how the mechanics of a true, living hope operate!

"Blessed is the nation whose God is the LORD: and the people whom he hath chosen for his own inheritance."[9] Blessed are you who *fully* place your hope in God. *Not* in man. *Not* in a friend that resides in America, Canada, Britain, Germany, Japan or Australia! *Not* in a rich and powerful connection – *but in God!*

Blessed are you too, when the 'roving' eyes of the Lord find you – and single you out for *His* favor![10]

> *"Thus saith the Lord; Cursed be the man that trusteth in man, and maketh flesh his arm, and whose heart departeth from the LORD."*

—JEREMIAH 17:5

As a wife, even though you expectantly hope to be cared for and looked after by your husband – and those needs are perfectly legitimate; yet, he is *not* your essential Source upon whom *your* hope and anchor rest! God is! Never attempt to place your spouse's bottom on God's throne; that would be tantamount to sheer idolatry!

Would you please reckon with me that converse to the 'fleshly-arm hopeful' is the experience of that 'Godly-arm hopeful' – that person whose essential, expectant hope is *fully* secured in God, alone:

> *"Blessed is the man that trusteth in the LORD, and whose hope the LORD is."*

—JEREMIAH 17:7

Is the LORD, your sole, expectant Hope?

If you must arise from this "pit of despair" – these *valleys of despondency, disgrace and destitution*, God has to be

FOUR PROVEN, LIFE-SUSTENANCE PRINCIPLES

the only One upon Whom your total hope, expectations and desires rest!

3. *Remember to Wait for the Lord's Rescue Plan, Alone*

"Multitudes, multitudes in the valley of decision ..."

—JOEL 3:14

Long ago in 835BC when Prophet Joel had commenced his prophetic ministry – just a little above two centuries before Prophet Jeremiah – Judah had been in the middle of a buoyant, prosperous and plentiful economy that had eventually proven to be her undoing, leading her heart away from the God! Her citizenry had eventually begun sliding gradually downwards. That rebellious backslide had tail-spun her into complacency and self-centeredness.

Joel had prophesied in Judah for almost a generation – thirty-nine years to be exact – pleading with God's people to return to Him. Those prophecies and pleas had fallen on deaf ears. As a result, God had promised to visit her with His judgment. One of the visions of judgment the prophet had received of God had been that of an innumerable, countless *"multitudes in the valley of decision"* (Joel 3:14).

Now, there's a pronounced characteristic commonly shared by the "multitudes" in *any* 'valley', ir-respective of geographical location and/or cultural diversification: *a confusion that beclouds a genuine sense of right direction and judgment!*

Remember, the *'valley'* represents the location of 'molting experiences'; the *very* depths of despair, despondency, rejection, loneliness and dejection. Oh, it is pretty easy to become rattled in the *'valley'*. It is a common sight to find a conurbation of weakened bald eagles in the valley – once buoyant and majestic in flight – stumble and fall upon each other due to poor, restricted visibility, exhaustion, dehydration and/or lack of stamina, once molting sets in!

In the *'valley'* abide hunger, deprivation and starvation.

In the *'valley'* exists restricted vision/visibility.

From the *depths of the valley* – because of a distorted view from an impossible viewing angle of elevation – everything else above the molting eagle seems gigantic, whilst he feels most inconsequential!

Back to human scenery now, the "multitudes" in the *valley of life* are synonymously symbolic of those count-

FOUR PROVEN, LIFE-SUSTENANCE PRINCIPLES

less thousands upon the earth, undergoing – at least – *one* unpleasant 'molting' experience.

Because their minds are boggled to such an undefinable state of remote confusion, *valley-dwellers* who have imbibed *'valley mentality'* may *not* be able to easily configure a potential 'way of escape', out of their troubles.

This is *why* this book has been penned: *just for you!*

I have confided in you, two life-sustenance principles that will translate unto 'ways of escape' out of *any* trouble; I'm just about to place at your reach, the third: *remember to wait, patiently for the Lord's rescue plan, alone!*

Prophet Jeremiah had written:

> *"The Lord is good unto them that wait for him, to the soul that seeketh him."*
>
> —LAMENTATIONS 3:25

In the depth of despair in the *"valley"*, you must continually assure – and re-assure your soul, "I am serving *the* faithful God!"

WHEN THE CHIPS ARE DOWN

Why must you do this?

You must continually assure – and re-assure your soul, "I am serving *the* faithful God" because, it is in the *"valley"* it is easiest to start believing the "sweet-nothing" whispers of the devil, the enemy of your soul. It is at such a time as this, surrounded by other 'bare' creatures that you are most prone to become discouraged, disillusioned and distressed in the "spirit of your mind."

It is in the *"valley"* that you find people who had once been entirely set free from bondages and/or addictions begin to crave for the same old addictive behavioral lifestyles, again. Once sharp battleaxes of the Lord now find excuses to revert to rustiness and bluntness; they would soon begin to shy away from upright discerning friends and associates who would otherwise have held them accountable, questioned their ir-reverent acts and shaken that *stupid* complacency off them!

It is in the *"valley"* that hitherto men and women of power in the Spirit become so *"weak like anyone else"* – so easily overwhelmed, frustrated, discouraged – and overcome by little, almost insignificant matters of life![11]

It is in the *"valley"* when the *chips are down* that the liar, the devil – and his demons clutter-chatter the loudest, in

FOUR PROVEN, LIFE-SUSTENANCE PRINCIPLES

people's cochleae in an ever so successful campaign-trick to muffle the voice of the Spirit!

But equally important it is to mention that it is in the midst of the disequilibrium of the *'valley'* you ought to awaken the "spirit of your mind" and realize you *own* the responsibility to see to the welfare of your very soul – to *patiently* wait upon the faithfulness of the living God!

Any faithfully awaiting God's faithfulness wouldn't hatch neither scheme *another* potential "way of escape". They know it too well, that such scheming won't work! Neither will it bring them to the mountaintop, but should instead sink them deeper, into the mires of despair – that is, if they survived *the* imminent crash!

Similarly, a wise driver wouldn't show off any 'Fast 'n Furious' motoring skills on a foggy, wet and snowy day. There's no such need as to become desperate in convincing anyone on how good a driver you are on such a wet day on such an icy road! Rather, you would kill your speed, dead! Very well *'dead'* below the speed-limit sign: that's what the *Driving Agency* would request of you at such times.

Why?

WHEN THE CHIPS ARE DOWN

Because visibility is drastically reduced – and if you disregard motoring ordinances and advice, you may likely cause harm to yourself and/or other road users!

A young lady had been jilted by a guy she had been engaged to, a couple of weeks to their proposed wedding. Her mind hadn't been able to quite absorb the unexpected, sudden, adverse twist of events. She had been admitted into the hospital under the legal holding of the *Mental Health Act, Section* 3; *(England & Wales)*. This meant her affairs *had* required to be advised upon and supervised by the specialists under the auspices of the government's department of mental health – for up to six months at first; renewable, if need be for another half year, at least!

She would remain "under care" – until she had been periodically assessed. Within that initial six-month assessment and treatment limit, if they – the specialists – deemed her fit for release, they would advise her lawyer/solicitor and also the court, presided upon by a judge! She would be presented before the judge, who, based upon the evidence(s) produced in her paperwork by the legal and health counsels shall release her to her parent(s)/legal care-giver/next of kin chargeable with the sole responsibility of "keeping a watchful eye" on her health, just in case it deteriorates!

FOUR PROVEN, LIFE-SUSTENANCE PRINCIPLES

Barely five weeks after her release, she had met and fallen in love with another young professional man – and had announced an engagement party!

Honestly, I had felt the entire plan had been too drastic – after all, there's a "minimum" required standard set in *"Zion for a foundation, a stone, a tried stone, a precious corner stone, a sure foundation; he that believeth shall not make haste."*[12] I'd duly informed her family that I'd thought she would have fared well to have taken a break from dating, entirely, for at least six months up to a year, found herself a trade or a job and settled in gradually back into the pressures and routine of daily living! My advice had fallen on a few pairs of deaf ears in the family because I'd confirmed in the mail, a formal invitation to the engagement party!

I'd forwarded a beautiful, white *'Congratulations on Your ENGAGEMENT'* card: I couldn't bear to bring myself to honor such party with *my* presence!

As I had later gathered from reliable sources many months thereafter, the aftermath of the party had been a case of "history repeating itself": broken engagement, no marriage – and a replay of the vicious circle!

WHEN THE CHIPS ARE DOWN

You probably know *why* that lady's story had turned out so drastic, don't you?

The reason is simple: dwellers in the *'valley of molting'* would yet dare 'lift off', soar, or dive all too prematurely – or too suddenly. Their thought patterns defy spiritual logic which Prophet Jeremiah had rightly sign-posted:

"PATIENTLY WAIT ON GOD!"

Apostle Peter had admonished his readers:

> *"Be sober, be vigilant; because your adversary the devil, as a roaring lion, walketh about, seeking whom he may devour:*
>
> *Whom resist steadfast in the faith, knowing that the same afflictions are accomplished in your brethren that are in the world."*

—1 Peter 5:8-9

People who are sober do *not* tear ahead in the fog. Neither do they enforce God to rubber-stamp their fleshly plans!

Sober drivers have *nothing* to prove to other drivers – or indeed, road users!

FOUR PROVEN, LIFE-SUSTENANCE PRINCIPLES

Sober minds do *not* yield to the temptation to resort to manipulating God or others into achieving their objectives, plans and purposes!

People who eventually arise from the "pit of despair" do *not* do so in their own strength or technical 'know how'. They neither gather pity-parties *nor* ferment schisms in order to advance and better their lot!

You see, adopting any of those modes of operation is tantamount to endorsing the *'valley-culture'*! It may yield you some temporary, short term 'results' based on the amount of exertion you selfishly input, in order to achieve those 'results'. In the long run however, those foul efforts eventually lead to prolonging your tenure in the "valley". They will prove to be wasted efforts that yielded wasted, corrupt fruits unable to withstand the test of time – filling you with utter frustration and despair!

Frustration and despair are a couple of so many reasons people *cannot* think wholesome thoughts but rather commit suicide, abuse chemical substances or treat fellow beings with such outrageous, demeaning behaviors!

People who are patiently waiting upon the Lord's intervention, however, are rid of 'valley mentality and culture'! Instead they are sober – and vigilant!

WHEN THE CHIPS ARE DOWN

Sobriety calls for *vigilance* and *watchfulness*. This is the attitude Christ expects of His Church, His Bride at His coming! She *must* be sober-minded if she would *not* miss *her* Bridegroom!

Sober minded people are *watchful*; watchful for the performance of the promises of God which they have laid hold upon, in the spirit of an *expectant, living hope* that fails not, neither makes ashamed.[13]

Sober minds are *zestful*; they give God *no* rest in their daily supplications, intercessions and giving of thanks until He performs His promises promised them, which they have laid hold upon in *'rhema'* form!

Sober saints *solidly build upon the foundation laid in Zion*; they are never in an hazardous haste trying to accomplish *a* thing for God's glory – or theirs!

Sobriety causes for a *hopeful encouragement* of one's heart in the Lord!

> *"I had fainted, unless I had believed to see the goodness of the LORD in the land of the living.*
>
> —PSALMS 27:13

FOUR PROVEN, LIFE-SUSTENANCE PRINCIPLES

After having waited patiently for the salvation of the Lord, you are assured to rise again. You shall mount up with new wings like a rejuvenated, 'molted', bald eagle!

Prophet Isaiah had prophesied:

> *"But they that wait upon the LORD shall renew their strength; they shall mount up with wings as eagles; they shall run, and not be weary; and they shall walk, and not faint."*

—ISAIAH 40:31

Furthermore, prophet Jeremiah exposed unto us, a neatly tucked-away secret:

> *"The LORD is good unto them that wait for him, to the soul that seeketh him.*
>
> *It is good that a man should both hope and quietly wait for the salvation of the LORD."*

—LAMENTATIONS 3:25-26

The Psalmist had exposed the secret of his rejuvenated strength. He had penned:

> *"I had fainted, unless I had believed to see the goodness of the LORD in the land of the living.*
>
> *Wait on the LORD: be of good courage, and he shall strengthen thine heart: wait, I say, on the LORD."*

—Psalms 27:13-14

4. Remember to Abide under the Terms of your Character Development Exercise

Lastly, the prophet had argued:

> *"It is good for a man that he bear the yoke in his youth."*

—Lamentations 3:27

What *yoke* had Jeremiah advocated?

It was the *yoke* of the Lord!

"Oh, does the Lord have a yoke?", you ask!

Oh, sure yes; He does!

FOUR PROVEN, LIFE-SUSTENANCE PRINCIPLES

And before I go any further, I must clarify this *'yoke of the Lord'* is *not* sickness, affliction, hardship, poverty and penury. Nor is it a deluge of solution-defying problems. No; to the contrary, these are the yokes of the devil – for the enemy of your soul possesses in his arsenal a thousand-and-one of such with which to afflict!

Those demonic afflictions the Psalmist had rightly ordered: *"Lift up your heads, O ye gates; and be ye lift up, ye everlasting doors; and the King of glory shall come in"* (Psalms 24:7). Those are the *yokes* the anointing of the Holy One seeks to destroy, irreconcilably! (Isaiah 10:27).

But God doubtless has His 'ready yokes' for the necks of His children! I know this is true because Abraham had been prosperous – yet had *had* to pay a ready *price* in his walk of faith with the Almighty. God's instruction to Abraham to *"Walk before me, and be thou perfect"* had become his *yoke!*[14]

God's call to "walk before me, perfect" isn't any different a call to our generation today. This invite from Father God – to don His yoke, if obediently accepted by His children – produces a staggering, astonishing effect. It produces an exertion-force, which bears witness to a gradual, daily death of their fleshly nature! The marks left by His *yoke* can be easily noticeable to the keenest eyes of families and friends who may be censorial of their daily walk of obedience, with God. God's yoke therefore sometimes becomes a hidden, yet significant glaring spiritual ornament upon their *spirit-man!*

The Lord Jesus Christ issued the same invite to *anyone* troubled, discouraged, despondent or afflicted; in short, to *any* who dwells in the *'valley of molting.'* Here reproduced are His exact words:

> *"Come unto me, all ye that labour and are heavy laden, and I will give you rest.*
>
> *Take my yoke upon you, and learn of me; for I am meek and lowly in heart: and ye shall find rest unto your souls.*
>
> *For my yoke is easy, and my burden is light."*
>
> —MATTHEW 11:28-30

This *'yoke of the Lord'* is that light pressure He exerts upon the *"soul-spirit"* of all those who are willing to "walk before Him, perfect!" Their yieldedness eventually translates into a changed, more-refined character of obedient, willing, yielded saints.

FOUR PROVEN, LIFE-SUSTENANCE PRINCIPLES

Drop to the bare ground, that generalized name "christian"; anyone could conveniently refer to themselves as such yet, without ever having encountered the savoring experience the richness of God's *"Character Development Exercise"* earns. This was one huge reason Paul the apostle had written an entire volume to the Romans.

In *Romans 5:2-5*, he had re-assured his readers with these words:

> *"By whom also we have access by faith into this grace wherein we stand, and rejoice in hope of the glory of God.*
>
> *And not only so, but we glory in tribulations also: knowing that tribulation worketh patience;*
>
> *And patience, experience; and experience, hope:*
>
> *And hope maketh not ashamed; because the love of God is shed abroad in our hearts by the Holy Ghost which is given unto us."*

At least *two* resultant effects are glaring in the passage of scriptures above:

- First, the tribulations you face for the sake of the Gospel and/the Lord of the Gospel usually produce *patience* – a rare virtue without which no person survives the *"valley"* experience nor indeed, that of an exalted plane. In other words, if you lacked God-induced patience but managed by dint of self-effort or otherwise to gather much, you will soon fall to the bottom of the *"valley"* where you would now, somehow, be enlisted in any of life's bitter *Character Reformation Exercises!* Trust my prophecy!

Patience is *not* a gift. It is a *fruit* – one of the essential "fruits of the Spirit." Fruits can only be borne by a viticulture that has undergone supervised cultivation and pruning!

- Second, as *patience* does *his* work, your spiritual nature is translated within those very intrinsic processes. This 'new personality' emerging from such rigorous turns of events ultimately results into your *earthly recognition* and also, *eternal glory!*

Apostle Peter encouraged his readers to cultivate, with all diligence, a deliberate exercise and development of their faith, virtue, knowledge, temperance, patience, godliness, brotherly kindness and love. Says he:

> *"For if these things be in you, and abound, they make you that ye shall neither be barren nor un-fruitful in the knowledge of our Lord Jesus Christ.*

FOUR PROVEN, LIFE-SUSTENANCE PRINCIPLES

But he that lacketh these things is blind, and cannot see afar off …"

—2 PETER 1:8-9

That last line in the Apostle's writing reflects summarily, a person in the *'valley of molting'*: they *cannot* – and do *not* see afar off!

God is *not* unrighteous as to forget your existence to the "School of Character Development" forever; you're in there *only* for a season – a stipulated period of time. Endeavor to ensure you enduringly bear *"the yoke"* with an expectant hope, patience and a deliberate co-operation, His processes of emerging that desired *new* nature in you, by His Spirit!

"For the Lord will not cast off for ever:

But though he cause grief, yet will he have compassion according to the multitude of his mercies.

For he doth not afflict willingly nor grieve the children of men."

—LAMENTATIONS 3:31-33

Any person who puts these great *four* principles of life-sustenance into practice should not be barren in rescuing themselves or other wounded eagles out of the *"valley of despair"*.

I pray that person is *you!*

5

THE UNGRATEFUL SON

Now, for you who do *not* have a relationship with the Heavenly Father, I may best liken you to the *Prodigal son* whose story Jesus had related in Luke 15; a reckless, fun-loving young lad who had come to the end of his roads. His *'chips had come down'*!

He had been raised in a loving, affluent family – but that had proven to be lesser than 'lowest' on his ranking of priorities: he had *not* watched his influences.

Wild stock. Nonchalant. Arrogant attitude. Wild parties.

Inordinate spending – coupled with an affluent, ostentatious lifestyle had been his undoing.

Possibly drugs too, weren't lacking!

WHEN THE CHIPS ARE DOWN

Anyway, he'd abused his father; and with a roughshod attitude – possibly at knife or gun point had demanded his inheritance from him. Unbelievable as it may sound, his request had been speedily granted.

How many young people do you know who seemed to have all they ever wanted at the snap of two fingers – yet had lost it all within the blink of an eye?

His ingratitude and greed had taken him on a journey to a faraway destination. He had seemed to have forgotten his father's teaching that *"You only take a peek at the world, a view at a time; you never see the world at someone else's expense lest the world view you at your expense!"*

In the faraway country, he'd mingled with equally lousy batch of friends. They all had continued exploring their lavish lifestyles – until they had begun to be in want. Any person can tell who their *true* friends are *"when the chips are down."*

His friends had begun to leave him to his fate, one after the other. The wild sex and the drinks had become more and more dis-satisfying, the more he had engaged. Eventually the loud music too had soon died down!

THE UNGRATEFUL SON

No more swagger, no more 'bling-bling' gold – he'd pawned them all off, ever so cheaply! He had begun to be in dire lack – until he had joined up with a citizen. That citizen had him sent onto a hog-farm yard as a hired laborer. There he had fed the hogs – and he would *"gladly have fed on and filled his belly with the carob pods"*, but nobody would even offer anything of such dainty to him![1]

Someday, he had *had* enough!

Jesus said, *"he came to himself."*[2]

> *"Then when he came to himself, he said, How many hired servants of my father have enough food, and [even food] to spare, but I am perishing (dying) here of hunger!"*
>
> —LUKE 15:17;
> Amplified Version

How many in the world out there are famished in their spirit – and pining out?

That junction of 'coming to himself' – in other words, of 'coming to his right mind' and to terms with the magnanimity of his Father had changed his life forever!

WHEN THE CHIPS ARE DOWN

You too may possibly need to come to terms with the sure mercies of the Heavenly Father today, in order to escape the pigpen lifestyle you have chosen!

His sure mercies are extended, still. Don't refuse Him!

Pray this simple prayer – aloud, wherever you may be, right away:

> *"Dear Lord Jesus,*
>
> *I am at my wits' end. I hereby do open the door of my heart unto You, now; please come in. Forgive me my sins. Cleanse – and save me!*
>
> *And please write my name in the Book of Life.*
>
> *Thank you so very much!*
>
> *Amen!"*

If you prayed that prayer from your heart – and by faith, you've become a saved child of God. Write me today: N-O-W. I simply can't wait to read from you.

Write: '*reverendsammy@harvestways.org*' today!

Congratulations!

References

Preface

[1] *Ephesians 2:4*

Chapter 1

[1] *Stone Cold; Robert Swindells, Published by Puffin Books 1995, Printed in England by Clays Ltd, St Ives plc; ISBN 978-0-14036251-0*
[2] *Psalms 91:3*

Chapter 2

[1] *Psalms 35:27*
[2] *Collins Concise Dictionary, 21st Century Edition*
[3] *Judges 16:17; LIFE Application Study Bible Translation*
[4] *1 John 5:18*
[5] *John 10:10*

Chapter 3

[1] *Romans 2:20 & 1 Corinthians 3:1*
[2] *1 Corinthians 2:5*
[3] *Hosea Chapters 2 & 3*
[4] *Job 2:9-10*
[5] *Read Revelation 12:7-13*
[6] *1 Peter 1:7*
[7] *Revelation 4:1*
[8] *Hebrews 12:1; My rendition.*
[9] *Hebrews 2:10*
[10] *Colossians 2:14-15*
[11] *Exodus 20:2*

Chapter 4
1. *Psalms 124:7*
2. *Ephesians 2:1*
3. *Jeremiah 38:11-13*
4. *Zechariah 9:12 & Psalms 69:33*
5. *Psalms 103:1-5*
6. *Isaiah 43:26*
7. *Psalms 50:15*
8. *Hebrews 6:10 & Proverbs 19:17*
9. *Psalms 33:12*
10. *2 Chronicles 16:9*
11. *Judges 16:17; LIFE Application Study Bible Translation*
12. *Isaiah 28:16*
13. *Romans 5:3-5*
14. *Genesis 17:1*

Chapter 5
1. *Luke 15:16; Amplified Version*
2. *Luke 15:17*

Worship with Us

The Harvestways Int'l Church, (Birmingham, U.K.)	**The Harvestways Int'l Church (Nigeria, West Africa)**
Holloway Hall, Northfield, Birmingham England, B31 1TT, UK	1 Harvest Way, Off Elewura St. Behind GLO Office, Challenge, G.P.O Box 2910, Dugbe, Ibadan, Nigeria
Sundays: 12 noon- 2pm Fridays: 7–8.30pm	
Tel: (+44) 7854675159	Sundays: 9am Wednesdays: 6pm
admin@harvestways.org	*ngr.admin@harvestways.org*

You may want to inquire about SJM, invite Rev. Sammy to minister for you, please contact:

Sammy Joseph Ministries
P.O. Box 15129, Birmingham,
West Midlands, England, B45 5DJ

Mobile: (+44) 7854 675159

Other Books by the Author

Other books by the author that can be ordered at all Christian bookshops near you, *Pulse Publishing House* or from our website *www.harvestways.org* include:

APPRECIABLE Gifts

Seekers in quest of attaining inner peace with the heavenly Father, deepening satisfaction in their friendships/ relationships, healings from life's brokenness – enhancing their sexuality and marriages need search no further. Within the pages of *Appreciable Gifts* lie your missing trophies!

Irrespective of your status in life, if your heart desires to learn the most essential tips on how to 'spruce up' your 3-D relationships: vertical, horizontal and downwards, '*Appreciable Gifts*' will show you how! Read about: *The Greatest Gift of All, The Gift of Restoration, The Gift of a True Friendship, The Gift of Sex & Sexuality in Committed Relationships, and; Cultivating the Gifts of Thanksgiving & Gratitude.*

Read and apply guideposts on the parameters of offering, accepting, cherishing, maintaining – and abounding in gifts! The messages therein will positively impact your relationships for a lifetime!

(183 pages)

DESTROYING the Power of DELAY

This book is an expository piece of work, written in a scriptural, thought-provoking style. The author aimed at sharing with you from more than fifteen years of counseling in ministry, how to avoid the endearing long arms of delay; and if you're already entangled in a wild romance with the hated alien, the quickest way of escape from him.

Furthermore, real-life issues such as *'Causes of Delay'*, *'Who Should Care for the Elderly?'*, *'Wisdom Handling Inextricable Covenant Relationships'*, *'Liberating Financial Management and Dealing with Indebtedness'* are adequately discussed. Others topics include: *'How to Effectively Handle Mid-life Crisis, Depression, Barrenness'* - et cetera!

(220 pages)

GIDEON: *Releasing the Potentials Within You*

This book draws analogies from the life of Gideon (one of Israel's Judges) and applies them to how you can effectively release the hidden potentials within you. Written in easy, straightforward, simple language, you will find basic practical insights that will help lift you above common mediocrity levels in life!

(176 pages)

Before You Step Into Someone Else's Shoes

This book contains *easy-to-do* guides on how you will not repeat the costly mistakes made by others faced with a fresh opportunity to begin anew after suffering a heavy setback. We have also provided essential checklists to anyone willing to *step into shoes* ordained of God for them – as well as checkmating the mutineers!

(46 pages)

Become a Vision Partner with Sammy Joseph Ministries

Our commitment is to:

- Pray - and cover you daily in prayers, that God's undeniable blessings be upon your you and your household.
- Keep ministering the Word of God diligently.
- Minister to you once a month in a personal letter from Rev. Sammy Joseph - plus a telephone call from us.
- Issue you an official partner certificate.
- Offer you from time to time, special gifts for your spiritual growth and upliftment.

Your commitment is to:

- Pray for us always.
- Be committed to support our broadcasts/meetings in your area.
- Support us financially with your monthly 'seed' as said in Philippians 4:17.
- Always speak positive words of affirmation on the ministry, Rev. Joseph – and his family.

If you would love:

- To join or help us plant a branch of *The Harvestways Int'l Church* in your region;
- Become a vision partner/supporter of *Sammy Joseph Ministries*;
- Become a volunteer at any of our outreaches.

Please contact us at our addresses, today.

Contact Addresses

United Kingdom

Sammy Joseph Ministries
Box 15129
Birmingham,
England, U.K
B45 5DJ
Tel: 07854675159
Tel: 07758195466

pulsepublishinghouse@harvestways.org

Nigeria

Pulse Publishing House
Plot 1, Harvest Way
Behind GLO Office
Challenge
G.P.O. Box 2910
Dugbe, Ibadan
Nigeria.

pulsepublishinghouse @harvestways.org

PULSE Publishing House also avails you a secure processing and prompt
worldwide shipment of orders primarily via *www.harvestways.org*
Other leading outlets include *WHSmith.co.uk*, *Barnesandnoble.com*, *Amazon.com*

Notes

www.ingramcontent.com/pod-product-compliance
Lightning Source LLC
Chambersburg PA
CBHW031407040426
42444CB00005B/448